UNDERCOVER STORY

THE HIDDEN STORY OF
DRUGS

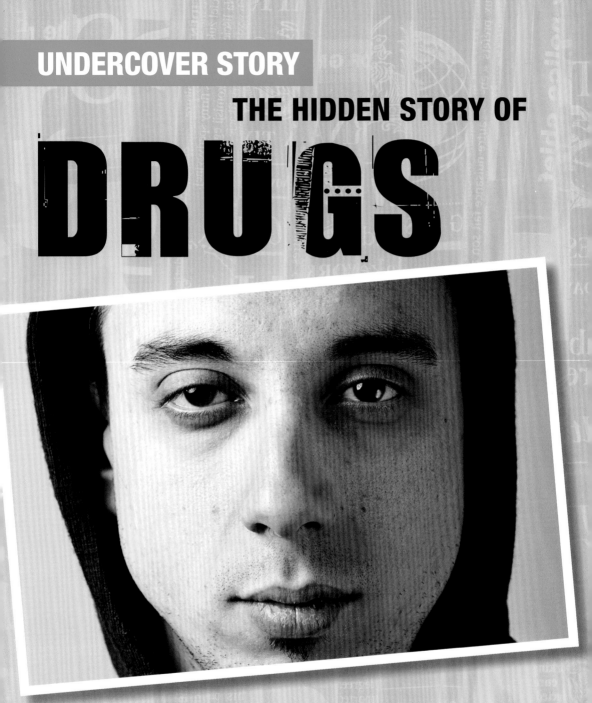

Karen Latchana Kenney

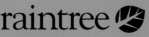
raintree
a Capstone company — publishers for children

Raintree is an imprint of Capstone Global Library
Limited, a company incorporated in England
and Wales having its registered office at
264 Banbury Road, Oxford OX2 7DY –
Registered company number: 6695582

www.raintree.co.uk
myorders@raintree.co.uk

Text © Capstone Global Library Limited 2016
The moral rights of the proprietor have been
asserted.

Produced for Raintree by Calcium
Edited by Sarah Eason and Jen Sanderson
Designed by Keith Williams
Picture research by Sarah Eason
Production by Victoria Fitzgerald
Originated by Capstone Global Library Ltd © 2016
Printed and bound in China

ISBN 978 1 4747 1635 2
19 18 17 16 15
10 9 8 7 6 5 4 3 2 1

British Library Cataloguing in Publication Data
A full catalogue record for this book is available
from the British Library.

Acknowledgements
We would like to thank the following for permission
to reproduce photographs: Dreamstime: Alex Raths
16, Andreblais 37, Barsik 14, BDS 26, Bdingman
36, Dndavis 17, Elenathewise 27, Karinabak 29,
Littleny 30, Luckybusiness 34, Margaretwallace
28, Micro10x 7, Monkey Business Images 20,
Oguzaral 18, Photographerlondon 43, Poco BW 19,
Sepavo 8, Triocean 4, Twoellis 6, William87 1, 25,
Wizzard 11, Yuri Arcurs 5, 10; Shutterstock: Avava
44, Diego Cervo 35, Aubord Dulac 22, Meunierd
12, Monkey Business Images 39, Martin Novak
32, Photographee.eu 23, Santibhavank P 42,
Wavebreakmedia 40.

Cover photographs reproduced with permission of:
Shutterstock: Elena Rostunova.

> Some words are shown in bold, **like this**. You can
> find out what they mean by looking in the glossary.

CONTENTS

WITHDRAWN

THE TRUTH ABOUT DRUGS

Almost everybody uses some form of drug. Some of these drugs are legal but others are illegal. Sometimes, people want to feel different. They might have a headache or a cold. They might feel emotions, such as sadness or anxiety, that they want to change. Drugs can make people feel different. They might be helpful, such as when asthma drugs help a person to breathe. However, drugs can also have really bad effects, such as when a driver crashes a car while under the influence of heroin.

Drugs are substances that affect how a person's body works. Once drugs get into a person's body, they go to the brain. This affects the brain's messages to the body. If a person feels pain, a drug can stop the brain's signal to feel pain in that part of the body. That is why a person can feel different after taking drugs.

DIFFERENT KINDS OF DRUG

Some legal drugs are used often and are fairly harmless, such as aspirin and caffeine. Alcohol and tobacco are also drugs. Legal drugs can be bought at a shop or pharmacy. A doctor can also prescribe legal drugs to a patient.

An inhaler contains a drug that helps someone with asthma to breathe better.

Caffeine is a fairly harmless drug that is used daily by many people.

Illegal drugs are drugs that the law does not allow people to possess. In some cases, doctors can prescribe these drugs in specific amounts. They are often highly addictive and damaging to the mind and body. Heroin, cocaine and methamphetamine, or meth, are three illegal drugs but these cannot be prescribed by a doctor.

Drug use can easily turn into abuse, and both legal and illegal drugs can be harmful. Drug abuse can ruin the lives of users and their friends and family. It can cause harm to a person's body and take control of their mind. Drug use also supports an illegal drug supply industry – one that involves criminals and gangs.

This book examines what drugs are, what they can do and how people using them can get help. From first use to **addiction**, drugs affect not only users, but also friends, family and society.

CHAPTER ONE

DRUG ABUSE

Josh was a pretty average teenager. He came from a normal family that was very caring and loving. His family moved around a lot because his father was in the army. Josh had a great childhood, though.

Prescription pills can have dangerous effects if misused or combined with other drugs.

In secondary school, things started to change for Josh. He was shy and found it hard to make friends. He felt left out and distant. Then he met an older group of friends. He started playing truant to hang out with them. He began smoking cannabis and drinking alcohol. Soon he was taking acid, mushrooms and cocaine. He did not seem shy anymore and people wanted to hang out with him.

BREAKING NEWS

>> For some people, drug use leads to prescription abuse. That is when someone takes a medication that has not been prescribed to him or her.

The drugs soon started taking control of Josh's life. He stole money from his parents to buy drugs. He lost weight and had bloody noses from snorting drugs. His addiction later led to some very hard drugs, including heroin and prescription pills. What started out as a small habit had become a life that revolved around getting and using drugs.

A COMMON STORY

Josh's story is not that unusual among drug users. Casual drug use can lead to addiction – from cannabis all the way to heroin. Drug addiction not only hurts the user, but it can also hurt friends and family. Besides being harmful, taking some drugs could give the user a criminal record. Drug users risk their health and they break the law to get high.

Many people abuse prescription pills, sometimes stealing them from the medicine cabinets of others.

In 2013, a United Kingdom study found that 6 per cent of Britons surveyed had abused prescription drugs. This is double the figure from 2008.

THE EFFECTS OF DRUGS

Different types of drug have different effects. Some seem to give people more energy, while others slow people down. Some are more harmful than others. Some of the most harmful drugs include heroin and cocaine. Let's take a look at the different types of drug and their effects.

Cannabis, which is also called weed and marijuana, slows down the brain, while certain pills speed up the brain.

Depressants: These drugs slow down brain activity. They can make a person feel relaxed, sleepy or un-coordinated. Some depressants include alcohol, **inhalants**, heroin and cannabis.

Hallucinogens: These drugs change what a person sees or hears. They can make a person **hallucinate** or see something that is not there or hear different sounds that do not exist. LSD and ketamine are hallucinogens.

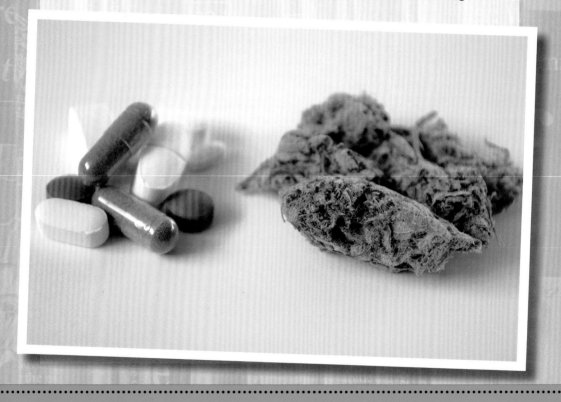

Opioids: These drugs are pain relievers. Some highly abused opioids are the prescription drugs codeine and methadone.

Stimulants: A stimulant increases brain activity. Users of these drugs feel that they have more energy and confidence. The caffeine in coffee is a mild stimulant. Cocaine and methamphetamine are much stronger stimulants.

Synthetics: These chemically made drugs mimic drugs such as cannabis, cocaine and methamphetamine. The drugs are sold in stores, but labelled for use in the bath or as incense. They are sometimes called "legal highs". Users have no idea what chemicals are in the mixtures, making them very dangerous. Some **synthetic** drugs include bath salts and spice. In the UK, there are plans to make all synthetic drugs illegal.

HITTING THE HEADLINES

MEPHEDRONE, A NEW DRUG

In the United Kingdom, mephedrone (also called meow meow), is one of the most used drugs among nightclub goers. Mephedrone was originally sold as a legal high and an alternative to stimulants such as speed, ecstasy and cocaine. To get around the law, dealers said that the mephedrone they were selling was plant food or bath salts. Mephedrone is a new drug so there is not a lot of information on its long-term use. The effects include euphoria, feelings of anxiety and **paranoia**. It can overstimulate the heart and nervous system, so it carries a risk of fits.

At first, many drugs make a person feel really good. They give the user feelings of confidence, energy or help him or her to relax. After a while, the drug wears off and the user "comes down". However, the user remembers the good feelings experienced when he or she first took the drug and wants to try that drug or other drugs again.

Taking drugs becomes a social thing. Users feel like they need the drugs to have fun. Other people might be using drugs at parties, too. They use together. Friendships form around drug use, but these are not healthy relationships. In a healthy relationship, people benefit from the relationship. In drugs-based friendships, there are no benefits.

Some people first try drugs at parties, thinking that they will have more fun.

BREAKING NEWS

>> A 2013/14 survey for England and Wales found that young adults were more likely to be frequent drug users than older people. The proportion of

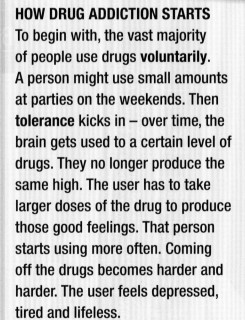

HOW DRUG ADDICTION STARTS

To begin with, the vast majority of people use drugs **voluntarily**. A person might use small amounts at parties on the weekends. Then **tolerance** kicks in – over time, the brain gets used to a certain level of drugs. They no longer produce the same high. The user has to take larger doses of the drug to produce those good feelings. That person starts using more often. Coming off the drugs becomes harder and harder. The user feels depressed, tired and lifeless.

Even the ritual of using the tools needed to take illegal drugs can become addictive.

Someone has become dependent on a drug when he or she needs it just to feel normal. The user now takes drugs every day, feeling an overwhelming need for the drug. The user does not care about the consequences of using and finds any way to get the drug, even if it means stealing or lying. This is drug addiction.

young adults aged 16 to 24 classed as frequent drug users was 6.6 per cent. In 2012/13, this was significantly lower at 5.1 per cent.

CHAPTER TWO

TEENS AND DRUGS

Lindsey was on her school swimming team and liked her French and art classes. She was not into drugs, but her boyfriend was. "I didn't drink, smoke weed or anything," she said.

Young people often feel under pressure from their peers to use drugs.

Her boyfriend used heroin. Soon Lindsey was using it, too. She started once every few weeks. Then she had to use every day. She stole money from her parents and lied about her addiction. Finally, she broke down and told her parents. She tried to quit but could not – Lindsey was hooked.

HITTING THE HEADLINES

PATTERNS OF DRUG USE

The 2013/14 Crime Survey for England and Wales (CSEW) interviewed a sample of 16-to-24-year olds. The survey found that in past year:

- 18.9 per cent had taken an illegal drug

- 15.1 per cent used cannabis

- 3.9 per cent used ecstasy

- 7.6 per cent had inhaled nitrous oxide

- 1.8 per cent had taken **salvia**. In the United Kingdom, the legality of salvia and other legal highs is still under review. Salvia has been banned in countries including Australia, Italy and Belgium.

When her class went on a field trip, Lindsey and a friend took drugs and needles. The school's staff found out and called Lindsey's parents. They came and took her home. Just two days before she was supposed to finish school, Lindsey was expelled. Lindsey used heroin, but that is just one kind of drug that teenagers abuse.

THE CANNABIS PROBLEM

Cannabis, or weed, is the most commonly abused drug by teenagers. It is often easily obtained and its effects are not always as long-lasting as those of other drugs. The problem of teenage drug abuse is growing, especially with prescription pills, synthetic cannabis and cannabis.

Being a teenager can be difficult. Bodies are changing. **Hormones** can cause emotional ups and downs. Social groups are growing and changing, too. Often for teenagers, it is hard to know how to act, make friends and fit in. Teenagers can feel extremely insecure and alone.

Unhappy teens may try drugs to hide their problems.

This is the time when many young people start experimenting with drugs. The average age young people first use cannabis is 14. Some teenagers stop soon after they try a drug. However, others continue using into adulthood, trying harder drugs over time. This is what leads to addiction.

REASONS FOR USING DRUGS

Teenagers start using drugs for many different reasons. They may try drugs to fit in with a group of peers, to feel more sociable. They may think that drugs will make them popular or better pupils or athletes. Some teenagers use drugs to concentrate better while they study. Some drugs help athletes to build muscles or run greater distances than others. Some teenagers have problems, such as sexual or emotional abuse, that they want to block out. Drugs make them feel numb and help them to forget. Others just want to rebel or even get attention.

A history of drug use in a family can also be a reason for a teenager to start using. They follow a pattern set by their parents or siblings. Watching their family use drugs makes it seem like a normal or even acceptable thing to do. Some teenagers learn to cope with their issues by using drugs. Some young people may suffer from **depression** or other mental health issues. They believe drugs will help them to overcome those problems.

The reality is that drugs do not solve problems. Once the drugs wear off, those same problems are still there.

HITTING THE HEADLINES

DIGITAL PEER PRESSURE

Online social networks add to the peer pressure exerted on teenagers. In a recent survey, 75 per cent of teenagers said that seeing photographs of young people doing drugs on Facebook or other social networking sites made them want to try drugs.

Drugs are not just bought in drug deals anymore. They are found at parties and other social situations with friends. They are found in medicine cabinets at the homes of friends and neighbours and bought online. Drugs are also found in schools. It is not too hard for teenagers to find drugs if they really want to. Teenage access to illegal drugs is widespread.

DRUGS AT HOME AND SCHOOL

Teenagers may also raid medicine cabinets of friends and neighbours to steal prescription pills. This can be very harmful, especially when they use drugs that they know very little about. Schools are one of the easiest places for teenagers to find drugs. A recent survey in the United States found that nearly 91 per cent of the pupils

Teens may fake symptoms to get drug prescriptions for illnesses they do not have.

BREAKING NEWS

>> Some pupils are abusing drugs not to get high, but to try to help them to do better in school. The prescription stimulant Ritalin helps those who have attention deficit hyperactivity disorder (ADHD)

Teenagers may use the internet to swap notes on drugs.

knew someone at school who sold cannabis. Around 24 per cent knew someone who sold prescription drugs and 9 per cent knew someone who sold cocaine.

DRUGS ONLINE

Teenagers are also buying drugs through illegal online pharmacies. This is a highly dangerous way to get drugs. Buyers have no idea what they are really getting when the drugs arrive. The drugs may not even be those advertised.

No matter how illegal drugs are bought, one thing remains the same – buying and taking them is breaking the law. Taking a pill that has been prescribed to someone else is also illegal. Teenagers caught possessing or selling drugs can be arrested and the legal consequences can be very serious. However, what drugs do inside the body can be much more dangerous.

and related problems with concentration and focus. Pupils may fake symptoms in order to get a prescription from their doctor. They may also know someone at school who sells or has a prescription he or she is willing to share.

The brain is the most complex organ in the human body. Once drugs are taken, that is where they head. Once drugs hit the brain, they start changing the way it works. The brain then sends mixed signals to the body.

Drugs interfere with the way a person's brain works. This is especially dangerous because teenagers' brains are not fully developed.

Drugs affect three areas of the brain: the brain stem, the limbic system and the cerebral cortex. Each area controls different functions of the body, from the senses and feelings of pleasure to breathing. To control these functions, the brain sends messages from one area to another. These messages are sent through **nerve cells**. Chemicals extend from one cell to another, letting the messages travel through the brain.

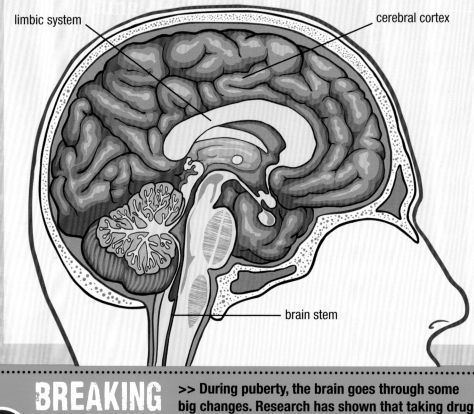

limbic system

cerebral cortex

brain stem

BREAKING NEWS

>> During puberty, the brain goes through some big changes. Research has shown that taking drugs during puberty may change how the brain grows.

SENDING MESSAGES

Some drugs mimic the chemicals that connect brain cells. They send abnormal messages throughout the brain and give users feelings of pleasure. Cannabis and heroin are two drugs that do this. Other drugs, such as cocaine and meth, interfere with the messages sent. They increase the chemicals sent between brain cells. This makes the messages have a much bigger impact than they normally would.

The good feeling or "high" that is made by drugs is created by the release of **dopamine** in the brain. Dopamine is a chemical that controls a person's emotion and pleasure. Drugs allow more dopamine to be released. The result of this is that the brain adjusts to the dopamine release so that when a person is not taking the drugs, it releases less dopamine than normal. This makes a person feel unhappy.

Once taken, drugs head straight to the brain.

Research also shows that addiction is a type of learning. If the brain learns to function on drugs, it makes it more likely that teenage users will later become addicts.

The mixed messages sent from the brain during drug taking make the body do unusual things. Drugs affect the senses and functions of the body.

Certain drugs cause hallucinations. Sometimes they are really scary, such as people or monsters attacking the user. Hallucinations can also make impossible acts, such as being able to fly, seem possible. Believing these hallucinations can cause people to do unsafe things. Sometimes, people jump out of windows or off buildings. Users can also become violent, imagining that others are trying to hurt them.

Stimulants increase a person's energy. They can make a user feel anxious, talkative and irritable. Stimulants also increase a person's heart rate and body temperature. Users lose their appetite when on the drug and can go without eating for a long time.

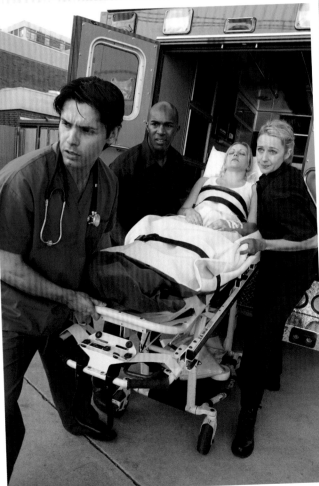

A drug overdose can cause serious health problems or even result in death.

SIDE EFFECTS

Different prescription drugs have varying side effects. Blood pressure and heart rate are raised with Dexedrine. Oxycodone can slow breathing. Some people have really dangerous reactions to prescription drugs. They can go into a coma, have seizures, and, in some cases, die.

Sometimes, teenagers mix drugs. The effects combine and multiply. This can lead to **dehydration**, loss of coordination, and breathing and heart problems. Mixing drugs can cause teens to stay high for long periods of time – even for hours or days. In some cases, the cocktail of drugs can lead teenagers straight to hospital.

UNDERCOVER STORY

DEADLY COMBINATION

In March 2012, English teenager, Drew Quinlan, was found face down on his grandfather's sofa, his jaw rigid and froth coming out of his mouth. At an inquest into his death, the coroner reported that Drew had 10 times the usual amount of the **anti-depressant** citalopram in his system. He also had morphine (which came from heroin) and one-and-a-half times the legal drink drive limit of alcohol. The inquest also heard that Drew's mother, father, uncle and aunt were all heroin users. They all, at some stage, had used the anti-depressant, and his aunt and uncle were still using it.

CHAPTER THREE

THE EFFECTS OF DRUGS

Megan had been sexually abused when she was younger. She had no idea how to deal with her problems. She wanted to cover up the pain in her life and thought that drugs might help. Megan was just 13 years old when she first tried drugs. First it was cannabis. Then she moved on to inhalants. Megan huffed (inhaled) anything she could find in the house.

Megan's parents thought something was wrong and sent her for counselling. She did not listen to her parents or therapist. Huffing was an escape from life for Megan. Her addiction soon grew out of control and Megan was huffing whenever she could. She no longer cared if anyone discovered her drug use. Her parents did find out that she had begun using again and she was sent to rehab.

Casual drug use can lead to a daily addiction.

BREAKING NEWS

>> In a survey published by the Health & Social Care Information Centre (HSCIC) in 2013, 5 per cent of 11-year-olds admitted to taking drugs but for 15-year-olds, this figure rose to 30 per cent.

Teenagers may take drugs to fit in with their friends.

It was during treatment that Megan realized, "Huffing could have killed me. I started to huff when I was 13 years old ... that's too young to do a lot of things, including becoming an addict or dying."

ABUSING FROM AN EARLY AGE
Just like Megan, many people begin abusing drugs as teenagers. They may have a history of drug abuse in their families. They may be trying to cover up painful memories. Some users may be trying to fit in with their friends. Drug use can start for many reasons but no matter how it starts, it will lead to problems.

At first, drug abuse is not always noticeable. Teenage drug users will often take drugs when their parents are not around and the effects wear off quickly. They may also work out really good ways to hide their drug use and they use excuses to explain their odd actions or moods. However, things quickly change as the drug addiction takes over.

HARD TO HIDE

A habit is harder to hide when the drug use occurs every day. Supporting a daily habit can be expensive, too. Teens do not usually have a lot of money available, so they find ways to get the money they need. They steal from family and friends or sell personal items to get cash. They take bigger risks, not caring about the social and legal consequences.

HITTING THE HEADLINES

FACES OF METH

The physical results of addiction can be very alarming. People change dramatically. It makes a big impact to see the physical toll drugs take on a person's body. A programme in the United States called The Faces of Meth shows a series of mug shots of meth addicts. The first photograph for each person is at an early arrest, while the second is at a later arrest. The differences are shocking. The later photos show people with sunken eyes and cheeks and scarred and scabbed faces. Meth mouth is also a disturbing result of meth addiction: meth causes broken, discoloured and rotten teeth. Meth stops saliva production, which allows acids in the mouth to eat away at the teeth. Users also grind their teeth and forget to brush or floss. It leaves the teeth looking black and worn down.

With daily drug use comes a physical and emotional toll. These are the signs to watch out for if you think someone has a drug problem:

- **Skipping out on responsibilities**: missing classes and work, getting bad results in school, not doing chores at home.

- **Increased risk taking**: driving under the influence, meeting up with strangers.

- **Legal trouble**: getting arrested, stealing.

- **Emotional issues**: fighting with family and friends, becoming more isolated from others, emotional highs and lows, anxiety and nervousness.

- **Physical signs**: sudden weight loss, bloodshot eyes, changes in sleeping patterns, picking at the skin and sores.

Drugs change how a person acts and looks.

Taking drugs can lead to some serious social problems. With an altered mind comes poor judgement. Users take risks by driving or going in cars while under the influence. On the road, they can kill themselves, passengers and other drivers in car accidents. drugs and risk taking

Teenagers who take drugs may be involved in violent situations. Under the influence of drugs, they put themselves in danger of being harmed by weapons or physical abuse. Young people on drugs take sexual risks, too. They may have unprotected sex resulting in a disease or pregnancy. They may also be photographed in the midst of risky behaviour. These photographs can make their way around social media, ruining a teenager's reputation.

Using drugs leads to bad choices, sometimes resulting in unplanned pregnancies.

BREAKING NEWS >> Studies have shown that those teenagers who have truanted or been excluded, were more likely to have tried drugs than those who had not truanted or been excluded.

DRUGS AND SCHOOL

If a teenager chooses drugs over school, the negative consequences may endure for years. They could change the teenager's academic and professional future. Drug use can lead to falling school marks, affecting what college or university will accept that teenager after they finish their final exams. Teenagers can be excluded if found using drugs at school, leaving them to find another way to finish school.

Drug use can end friendships, too. Users become isolated, spending a lot of time on their own. They stop answering phone calls and messages. Using becomes the most important thing in their lives. This can then lead to depression and loneliness. The most extreme result of these feelings is suicide.

Studying and tests can become less important to someone abusing drugs.

Drugs also have long-term consequences. If caught buying or selling drugs, a teenager can have lasting legal problems. Different countries have different laws, but most have strict laws relating to drugs. If convicted of a drug-related offence, the impact on a teenager's future can be great. He or she may not get the job applied for as an adult. He or she may not be able to join the armed forces or receive student loans, and may even have to serve time in prison.

Many homeless teens have drug-abuse problems.

A HISTORY OF ABUSE

Many young homeless teenagers have a history of drug abuse. They may become homeless because of their addiction or for other reasons. If they did not have a drug problem before living on the streets, they often develop one while on the streets. In 2012, UK charity Crisis said that 40 per cent of homeless young people were using drugs. Similar studies in the United States found that homeless youths are more likely than other teens to try crack, cannabis and other drugs.

HOMELESS AND HUNGRY PLEASE HELP

BREAKING NEWS

>> Homeless teens do not always become homeless because of addiction. However, living on the streets is stressful, scary and often dangerous. It can lead to drug addiction and mental health issues.

Drug abuse can lead users to commit crimes and spend time in prison.

Drugs can also cause long-term damage to the body. Some effects are unknown, but are being tested. Some animal tests show that ecstasy causes brain damage in animals. Inhalants break down a chemical in the brain. Over time, this can cause **tremors** and muscle spasms. Inhalants can also cause heart and liver damage. Stimulants can cause mental issues, such as paranoia and delusions. They can also make people lose their teeth and become anorexic. Different drugs do different damage, but they can all cause long-term and serious harm.

This, in turn, can result in risky behaviour and increase the chance of unsafe sex. When dealing with the basic problems of finding food and shelter, it becomes even harder to kick a drug habit. It is a vicious cycle for homeless teens.

CHAPTER FOUR

GETTING HELP

Sam first tried speed with some of her school friends. She liked it and began using regularly. It made Sam feel good and it also made her lose weight. That felt great because Sam had never liked her body. However, soon the speed was eating away at her life. Sam was fighting with her family. She was paranoid, too. She stayed in her room for days. Her weight dropped from 66 kilograms (146 pounds) to just 45 kilograms (99 pounds).

Fighting with family members could be a sign of drug abuse.

30

Sam started treatment nine months after she first tried speed. A few weeks later, Sam relapsed and used. She went on to relapse two more times. After being clean for 45 days, Sam was released from the rehab centre. She started seeing a therapist and moved back in with her family. Sam knew staying clean would not be easy, though. She had to go to her **group therapy** sessions at Narcotics Anonymous and stay away from bad influences. Being drug-free would take work for the rest of Sam's life.

STEPS TOWARDS RECOVERY

For addicts like Sam, detox and rehab centres are the first steps towards recovery. Getting off drugs is hard, but staying off them can be even harder. Most drug users relapse several times over many years. Each day is a constant battle to stay clean, but with the right support, former users can have happy lives without drugs.

UNDERCOVER STORY
WHY IS STOPPING SO HARD?

Drug-taking is difficult to stop and relapse is just a part of recovery. That is because addiction can be as much a mental condition as a physical one. Some people are ordered to go to treatment by the court or they are pressured by friends and family to go. They may not want to quit. Treatment can help a person stop using – but treatment is not a cure for addiction.

Getting help is the first step to stopping drug abuse. Help may be offered by friends and family. They stage an **intervention** with the user. An intervention is when friends or family confront someone who has an addiction. They offer their support to help get the user off drugs.

PHYSICAL AND MENTAL

Drug addiction is both a physical and mental problem. To get rid of the physical addiction, the body needs to release all of the drugs in its system. This is called detoxification or detox. This process is usually done at a detox centre. During detox, a person can experience terrible withdrawal symptoms, depending on the drug. Some of these symptoms include sweating, nausea and hallucinations. The symptoms are the result of the body getting the drugs out of its system. Doctors at the centre help the person safely get the drugs out of his or her system.

A friend's support can help save a drug user's life.

HITTING THE HEADLINES

GROUP THERAPY: A BAD INFLUENCE?

Sometimes rehab can be harmful, not helpful. A *Time* magazine article claimed that group therapy can be a bad influence for teens. The teens hear stories about drug use and may then want to try the drugs mentioned. "Many programmes throw casual dabblers together with hard-core addicts … Just putting kids in group therapy actually promotes greater drug use," said Dr Nora Volkow, director of the National Institute on Drug Abuse in the United States.

FINDING TREATMENT

After detox, the next step is a rehabilitation (rehab) or treatment centre. This is a centre with doctors, therapists and other drug users seeking recovery. The treatment for a drug addict can include therapy, which is talking about a person's problems. It helps a user to understand why he or she started using in the first place.

The person may have a problem that has never been resolved. Therapy can help the person deal with that problem. Medication can help a person to deal with mental health issues or remaining physical problems. Treatment can take a few weeks to several months. The length of treatment depends on the person's level of addiction.

Returning to normal life can be hard for someone just out of treatment. Old friends may be around and bad influences can tempt a teenager to use again. It is easy to fall back into bad habits. It is much harder to stay clean.

Having support helps former drug users to stay clean.

Support groups help teenagers to stay off drugs. These groups meet regularly. They are places where former addicts can discuss their temptations with people who have similar experiences and are facing the same challenges. Some groups are just for teenagers. It helps teenagers to know that they are not alone in their fight to stay clean.

BREAKING NEWS

>> In 2013 to 2014 in the United Kingdom, 19,126 people under the age of 18 accessed treatment for their addiction. Just over half (53 per cent) were aged 16 to 18 years.

Stress is a common risk factor for a drug relapse.

STUMBLING BLOCKS

Despite having the support of others, a relapse can happen to anyone. Relapses usually happen a few times during recovery. Certain things can trigger a relapse, such as being around others using drugs, boredom and isolation.

Mental or physical illness are other common triggers for relapses. Teenagers must know their triggers and do their best to stay away from them. That is the best way to prevent relapses. After a relapse, teens usually go back to a treatment centre.

CHAPTER FIVE

SOCIETY AND DRUGS

Many drugs are illegal in the United Kingdom. These illegal drugs are mostly used to get high. However, some drugs are used in different cultures for religious reasons or for medicinal purposes, in the case of cannabis.

Indian hemp is used in India for religious ceremonies. Some mushrooms cause hallucinations and are used by native peoples of Latin America. The native peoples of Mexico use mescaline (see page 37) for religious purposes.

In nearly half the states in the United States, medical cannabis is legal if it is given by prescription.

BREAKING NEWS

>> A whole industry has grown up around medical cannabis. In the United States, in states where it is legal, there are businesses that specialize in making products containing medical cannabis. These include lemon bars, drinks and sweets.

The peyote plant has been grown and used Mexico for thousands of years.

USES OF DRUGS

Mescaline comes from the peyote cactus. When its "seeds" are chewed, they cause hallucinations that can last for up to 18 hours. Another drug used in South America is believed to heal its users. It is made from the stem bark of certain vines. These drugs are used to enhance religious experiences. While these drugs are used ceremonially, it does not mean they are safe. They have the potential to harm a person's mind and body, especially if abused.

Cannabis is a plant that is usually smoked or eaten. It is thought to relieve pain, anxiety, nausea, anorexia, some eye problems and seizures. In 2010 in the United Kingdom, the drug Sativex®, which contains cannabis, was approved for use by sufferers of multiple sclerosis. In 2015 in the United States, the use of medical cannabis was legal in more than 20 states.

This industry makes a lot of money selling cannabis products to people with medical conditions. However, some people think that patients may not have true medical conditions. In the state of Colorado, 94 per cent of people with prescriptions had them for "severe pain", which is very difficult to measure or prove.

Schools are one of the most common places where teenagers buy and sell drugs. Some schools in the United Kingdom, Australia, Sweden and the United States test pupils for drugs. The schools select pupils who they believe could be using drugs and ask them to provide a urine sample to test.

Schools want to decrease drug use among pupils. If a pupil tests positive, interventions and treatment may be recommended to the pupil and his or her family. Early intervention is vital in preventing later drug addiction. Pupils can also be excluded from school for using drugs.

HITTING THE HEADLINES
CHALLENGING DRUG LAWS

There are some schools in the United Kingdom that test their learners for drugs, but the majority do not. While many schools were initially enthusiastic about testing, this excitement fell away when practically, schools realized that the testing would not fit the ethos of their schools, their budget or that the approach would prove to be ineffective in deterring pupils from drugs. New research says that instead of testing to deter teenagers from using drugs, schools should adopt a positive ethos. In this, schools work to develop pupils' attachment to school through things such as firm school rules, helping pupils to develop positive friendships with their peers, and fostering the sense that teachers care about their pupils. It is thought that this more positive environment will be more effective than drugs tests.

IS TESTING USEFUL?

Critics of random drug testing at schools say that the tests can be seen as an invasion of pupils' privacy. Those who oppose the tests have compared them to using closed-circuit television (CCTV) cameras to "spy" on pupils, saying that they undermine trust in the community. Although there has not been a lot of research done on the effectiveness of random drug tests, studies have found that the tests are creating a bigger problem. Pupils know that cannabis stays in the body for longer than some drugs so while there has been a decrease in cannabis use, there has been an increase in harder drug use. Some people believe that this testing is helpful because it deters pupils from ever trying drugs.

Most pupils do not take drugs at school.

Prevention is important in reducing drug abuse amongst teenagers and the media is a powerful tool for educating teenagers on the dangers of drug use.

FRANK is a confidential helpline for anyone concerned about drug use. On talktofrank.com there is a comprehensive A-Z of drugs, which looks at each drug in detail, including information on the drug, the law, as well as the drug's side effects. Questions can be submitted online and the website also has many personal accounts from drug users to make teenagers aware of the dangers of taking drugs.

By discussing their effects, pupils learn just how much drugs can hurt them.

HITTING THE HEADLINES

CAMPAIGNS AT WORK

The Home Office says 67 per cent of young people in a survey said they would turn to Frank if they needed advice. In 2011/12, 225,892 calls were made to the Frank helpline and 3,341,777 visits were made to the website. Drug use in the United Kingdom has gone down by 9 per cent since Frank was launched, but experts say much of this is down to fewer people smoking cannabis.

FACING UP TO DRUGS

The charity Addaction has joined forces with the Amy Winehouse Foundation to deliver a Resilience Education programme to 250,000 secondary school children across England. The project includes drug and alcohol education and support for young people affected by substance misuse. It works by creating an environment where pupils can talk freely and openly about their lives, and to people who are in recovery from their own drug and alcohol abuse. The programme works with parents and teachers, helping them to understand drug and alcohol use.

There are many programmes to educate teenagers about drugs. It is also important for parents to talk to teenagers about using drugs. Some teenagers may not be aware of the health problems drugs cause or the risk of addiction. Parents can be the best help for teenagers at risk of becoming addicts.

If teenagers grow up to be adult addicts, the cost to society can be huge. These costs include increased criminal activity. Adults with severe, drug-related mental health issues can negatively affect communities. Children also pay the price for their parents' addictions. Babies can be born addicted to drugs or with defects as a result of their mothers' drug use.

A baby can be born with a drug addiction if his or her mother used drugs while pregnant.

CRIMINALS AND DRUGS

Drugs and crime are linked. Offenders fill prisons and, while there, use drugs as well. It is estimated that in the United Kingdom, 35 per cent of those in prison have a drug addiction and 6 per cent become addicts once they are in prison.

Trafficking drugs is also a huge international problem. Drug trafficking is the trade of illegal drugs around the world. Often this trade is controlled by gangs.

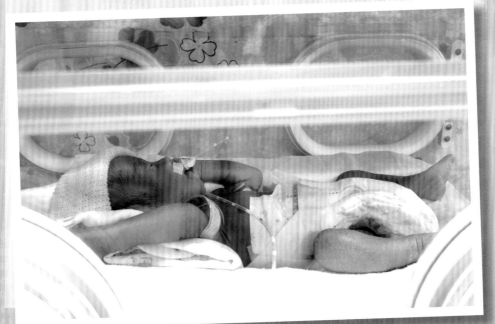

BREAKING NEWS

>> The financial cost to society as a result of drug abuse is significant. According to the NHS, each year, the overall cost of drug addiction in the

Prison time can be the consequence of illegal drug sales, purchases and use.

GANG WARFARE
Gangs use violence to resolve their issues with other gangs. This leads to deadly knifings of gang members and also innocent people caught in the fight.

Over time, drug addiction can also make mental health issues worse. Drug addicts with mental illnesses can be very difficult to treat. They may be hard to deal with, losing the support of families or groups. They may relapse often and need to be hospitalized.

Drug addiction can affect helpless victims. Drugs can cause birth defects in babies. These babies may have severely damaged brains. Addicts' babies can be born premature (before they are due), which can lead to many problems later in life. Addicts' babies can also be underweight or even die in the womb.

Drug addiction takes a toll on many people other than the addict and can cause problems throughout society.

United Kingdom is £15,400,000,000. The annual cost of drug-related crime is £13.9 billion and every year costs the NHS £488 million.

DRUGS - THE WHOLE STORY

The truth about drugs is that they affect many teenagers and can have devastating effects. Drugs may seem to be a way to escape life, but science shows that drugs just send mixed messages from the brain to the rest of the body. The teenage brain is still developing and can be permanently harmed by drug abuse. Drugs also have effects that make teenagers engage in risky behaviour, which can have terrible consequences. Once addiction takes over, the effects can cause permanent damage.

Without drugs, teenagers can live healthy lives.

HOPE FOR THE FUTURE

There is help for teenagers who abuse drugs, however. Treatment centres and support groups provide ways for young people to stop using and stay clean. Prevention is also very important. Learning about the effects of drugs may be all that a teenager needs to know to avoid drugs. Parents, teachers, friends and counsellors can provide support and advice for young people using or at risk of using drugs. The press can be an important tool, showing users what happens to the body and mind from drug abuse.

The teenage years are a crucial time to learn about the effects of drugs. Teenage users have a high risk of becoming adult addicts. Education and early intervention can stop that from happening.

UNDERCOVER STORY

A STORY OF RECOVERY

Lisa is 23. She has a home, a husband, a son and a stable job. But her life was not always this good. Her problems began when, at 12 years old, she started smoking cannabis. At 17, she found crack cocaine and by 18, she had a heroin addiction. After a phone call from her father, Lisa felt encouraged to escape life as a drug addict. She spent two weeks of abstinence at hospital and a further four months in therapy in residential rehabilitation. For Lisa, it was not just about fixing the problem quickly, but about the ongoing support to stay clean. She says, "I always use my support network and if I need to talk to somebody, their door will be open … I've got a fantastic life but I'm always going to be a recovering addict."

GLOSSARY

addiction when the body and mind crave and depend on particular substances, such as food, alcohol or drugs

anti-depressant prescription drug that can help someone suffering from depression to feel better

dehydration not having enough water in the body

depression mental illness that causes severe sadness

dopamine chemical in the brain that controls pleasure

group therapy support group in which people discuss their problems with other people who have the same or similar problems

hallucinate see things in the mind that do not really exist

hormone chemical made in the body that affects how a person grows and develops

inhalant substance that is inhaled (breathed in)

intervention action taken to improve or change a situation

nerve cell cell found in the body that conducts nerve impulses

paranoia irrational or unfounded feelings of mistrust and suspicion

prescription order for drugs written by a doctor to a pharmacist on behalf of a patient

salvia Mexican plant with leaves that contain chemicals that produce hallucinations when chewed or when dried and smoked

synthetic something that is made, rather than found in nature

tolerance lessening of a body's response to a drug

tremor shaking or trembling movement of the hands and legs or arms

voluntarily doing something willingly, not being forced to do something

FIND OUT MORE

BOOKS

A Little Book of Drugs: Activities to Explore Drug Issues with Young People, Vanessa Rogers (Jessica Kingsley Publishers, 2012)

Drug Crime (Inside Crime), Dirk Flint (Franklin Watts, 2010)

Keeping Safe Around Alcohol, Drugs and Cigarettes, Anne Rooney (Franklin Watts, 2014)

Why do People Make and Sell Drugs? (Global Issues), Anne Rooney (Franklin Watts, 2010)

ORGANIZATIONS

Frank
Helpline: 0300 123 6600
SMS 82111
Website: **www.talktofrank.com**
Frank is a drug awareness charity for anyone who needs to know more about a specific drug, its effects and the laws around the drug. Counsellors can help those facing an addiction or who have an addicted family member.

National Drugs Helpline
Helpline: 0800 77 66 00
The National Drugs Helpline is a 24-hour, seven-days a week, free and confidential telephone service that offers advice and information for those who are concerned, or have questions, about drugs.

Adfam
Adfam can help families dealing with drug abuse:
www.adfam.org.uk

NHS
The NHS Live Well pages have a lot of information on addiction support:
www.nhs.uk/Livewell/Addiction/Pages/addictionhome.aspx

INDEX